W9-AAS-982

Transportation and Travel

Joanne Suter

and

Susan M. Freese

L I F E S K I L L S™

H A N D B O O K S

21st CENTURY

Wieser Educational

30281 Esperanza
Rancho Santa Margarita, CA 92688-2130
1(800) 880-4433 ♦ Fax (800) 949-0209

www.wieser-ed.com ♦ Email info@wieser-ed.com

SADDLEBACK
EDUCATIONAL PUBLISHING
www.sdlback.com

Copyright © 2012 by Saddleback Educational Publishing
All rights reserved. No part of this book may be reproduced in any form or by any
means, electronic or mechanical, including photocopying, recording, scanning, or by
any information storage and retrieval system, without the written permission of the
publisher. SADDLEBACK EDUCATIONAL PUBLISHING and any associated logos are
trademarks and/or registered trademarks of Saddleback Educational Publishing.

ISBN-13: 978-1-61651-661-1
ISBN-10: 1-61651-661-5
eBook: 978-1-61247-349-9

Printed in Guangzhou, China
1111/CA21101811

16 15 14 13 12   1 2 3 4 5

Contents

Section 1   **Commuting to School and Work**   5

Chapter 1   Dangerous Travel and the Law   8

Chapter 2   Taking the "Ankle Express"   14

Chapter 3   Biking: The Rules of the Road   20

Chapter 4   Ride Sharing: Going My Way?   26

Section 2   **Traveling by Bus**   33

Chapter 1   The Benefits of Public Transportation   36

Chapter 2   Using a Route Map   42

Chapter 3   A Bus Schedule   48

Chapter 4   Easy, Economical Rides   54

Section 3   **Traveling by Train or Plane**   61

Chapter 1   The Benefits of Traveling by Train   64

Chapter 2   Buying Airline Tickets   70

Chapter 3   Reading a Flight Itinerary   76

Chapter 4   Overseas Travel   82

Section 4   **Planning a Vacation**   89

Chapter 1   Selecting a Travel Destination   92

Chapter 2   Planning Your Travel Budget   98

Chapter 3   Fly or Drive?   104

Chapter 4   Choosing a Hotel or Motel: 110
            Luxury or Economy?

Word List   116

Index   118

Commuting to School and Work

For most people, everyday travel means getting to school or work. Depending on where you live, you might have several choices of transportation. You can walk, ride your bike, or take a bus. Or maybe you can share a ride with fellow students or co-workers. In making your choice, you should consider not only convenience and cost but safety, too.

Making the Daily Commute

Andy had lived in the city all his life and never owned a car. He really didn't want to own a car, even though he could afford to now.

First of all, where would he park it? His neighbor, Sarah, owned a car. She had to run out and move it early every morning. Some mornings, Sarah drove around for 20 or 30 minutes. She spent a lot of time looking for new places to park. On weekends, she found it almost

impossible to find a spot within a block of the apartment. Sarah joked that moving her car was how she got her daily exercise. Not moving it meant getting an expensive ticket, though. The parking restrictions in the neighborhood were tough.

Second, where would Andy drive the car? He didn't want to drive to work every day. The plant where he worked was outside the city. It was a good hour's drive during rush hour—more during bad weather. Andy had found a ride share through his employer. One of his co-workers, Corey, lived only a few miles from his apartment. Corey picked Andy up and dropped him off every day for a reasonable fee. And along the way, they picked up another co-worker, Omar. The three had become pretty good friends over the year they had been sharing a ride.

CHAPTER **1**

Dangerous Travel and the Law

A roller coaster zooms up and down the hills and flies around the sharp corners. The riders' hearts pound with excitement.

Amusement park rides are amusing, because the riders aren't facing actual danger. Another kind of ride, however, is very dangerous indeed. "Hitching" a ride on a public highway puts people in real jeopardy.

rnational arrivals
ocal buses
Courtesy coaches
Tour coaches
Taxis

St
C·E
50 St · 49 St
N·R

42 St
ority
minal
A·C·E

Times Sq
42 St
7
N·R·S·1·2·3·7·9
34 St
Penn
Station

34
St
Herald

Enjoy a Sightseeing...

Hitchhiking

Standing by the roadside and trying to get a ride from a passing vehicle. The would-be rider usually sticks out his or her thumb or holds up a sign stating a destination.

Hitchhiking is not as common as it used to be. But some people still travel by "thumbing" a ride. Most hitchhikers are teens or young adults. They usually have little money to spend and a strong desire to get around. Online journals share stories of people hitchhiking all over the world.

Consequences

Do you think hitching is a cheap and easy way to travel? Think again. The cost of accepting a ride from a stranger can be high. Sometimes, thumbing a lift can have very serious consequences:

Horrendous

Terrible or horrifying.

→ According to one public safety official, "Some of the most *horrendous* crimes begin with the victim accepting a ride with a stranger."

Know the Laws!

Laws about hitchhiking vary from state to state. However, all of them are based on a national set of traffic rules called the *Uniform Vehicle Code* (*UVC*). According to the UVC, the act of hitchhiking is not illegal. However, where it can be done is restricted:

- Hitchhikers can't stand or walk on the roadway. If the roadway doesn't have a sidewalk, they must stay far enough away from the edge to be safe from passing cars. For instance, standing on the shoulder is considered safe.

- Some roadways, such as interstate highways, have *controlled access*. This means pedestrians can't enter them at all.

[FACT]

Hitchhiking
Loses Popularity

Hitchhiking reached its peak of popularity in the United States during the 1960s and 1970s. Since then, its popularity has dropped for three main reasons:

1. Most long-distance travel today is done on interstate highways. Hitchhiking on these roads is against the law.

2. Law enforcement officials pay closer attention to hitchhikers than they used to.

3. Many stories have been told about hitchhikers being assaulted and murdered. These stories have convinced people that hitch- hiking is dangerous.

→ The danger starts even before the ride begins. Hitchhikers that stand near or along a roadway risk being struck by a moving vehicle.

→ Hitchhikers are in more danger when they climb into a stranger's vehicle. They face the very real possibility of being kidnapped, robbed, assaulted, or even murdered.

→ Another danger concerns the driver. Hitchhikers don't know whether the person that picks them up has been drinking alcohol or taking drugs. Is this motorist in control of the vehicle? Of course,

What Do We Really Know about Hitchhiking?

Much of the information about hitchhiking has come from personal reports of riders and drivers. But that information isn't considered reliable, for two reasons. First, there's no way to determine whether these individuals' stories are accurate or truthful. And second, it's impossible to know whether these individuals' experiences were typical of hitchhikers overall. In general, people who support hitchhiking downplay the dangers associated with it. But people in law enforcement point to the crimes that occur among drivers and riders.

everyone runs the risk of being in a traffic accident every time he or she gets in a car. But the risk is obviously much greater for someone who knows nothing at all about the driver.

Drivers that pick up hitchhikers are also at serious risk. They don't know whether the smiling stranger standing on the side of the road is a good person or a criminal looking for a victim.

Safe Alternatives

There are better ways to share a ride than hitchhiking. Travel groups and agencies organize ride share programs that match riders and drivers. Shared rides can also be found using ride boards. These boards are often available at colleges and large workplaces. Yet another low-cost option is public transportation, such as a bus and train.

You'll get more details about economical transportation ideas as you read this book. It's possible to find transportation that's both inexpensive and safe.

Hitchhiking as "Russian Roulette"

A film produced by the US Department of Justice compares hitchhiking to playing Russian roulette. In that deadly game, individuals take their chances putting a loaded gun to their heads. The similarity to hitchhiking is that it's possible to thumb a ride or to give a ride without running into trouble. But the danger is always there. And sooner or later, people who give and get rides will probably become victims.

CHAPTER **2**

Taking the "Ankle Express"

Liza was tired of running for the bus and riding to school. So one day, she put on a pair of comfortable shoes and grabbed her backpack. She decided to take the "ankle express." Walking gave her an all-day physical and mental boost. She enjoyed taking in the fresh air and scenery and chatting with her neighbors and classmates.

Walking is the oldest and most basic means of transportation. When babies learn to walk, their world widens as they explore. But adults tend to lose their enthusiasm for walking. Also, some communi-

ties are not very "walkable." Many places are spread out. The people there depend on cars to get them to school, the mall, the library, and elsewhere.

Benefits of Walking

Walking—whether strolling or race walking—is an excellent way to maintain good health. It's simple, natural, and easy on the body. No expensive equipment or training is needed. And best of all, you can build muscle, strengthen bones, relieve stress, and improve your heart and lung function as you walk.

According to the US Surgeon General, physical activity doesn't have to be demanding to be healthy. Any moderate, regular activity—such as walking—can lower high blood pressure and help control weight. It can even reduce the risk of early death.

Do's and Don'ts

Walking is easy. But keep in mind these Do's and Don'ts:

→ **DON'T** walk at a pace that makes you breathe heavily. As you walk, you should be able to talk or sing without becoming breathless.

→ **DO** drink water or other fluids before, during, and after walking.

→ **DON'T** watch your feet while you walk. Doing so causes neck and shoulder strain. Walk with your head up, back straight, and shoulders relaxed. Also scan the sidewalk ahead for obstacles. Look for items in your path and broken or cracked pavement.

→ **DO** some stretching exercises before and after vigorous walking.

→ **DO** take smooth, even strides, even as you increase your speed.

→ **DO** vary your route to maintain interest and enjoyment.

→ **DO** wear comfortable, well-cushioned shoes and dress for the weather.

US Surgeon General

The US Surgeon General is sometimes referred to as "America's doctor." He or she is appointed by the president and serves a four-year term. The Surgeon General has the duty of "providing Americans the best scientific information available on how to improve their health and reduce the risk of illness and injury."

Types of Walking

- **Leisure walking:** Stroll at a light to moderate pace.

- **Race walking or power walking:** This form of walking comes close to running. To do it, pick up your pace and pump your arms.

- **Hill walking:** After walking on flat ground at a moderate pace for 5 to 10 minutes, walk up a hill at a steady pace. Then walk down the hill and back up again.

- **Interval training:** Start with a warm-up by walking at a light pace for 5 to 10 minutes. Next, walk as quickly as you can for 20 seconds. Then walk at a normal pace for 40 to 60 seconds. Continue to alternate between the fast and normal paces.

Walking as Cardiovascular Exercise

Walking is a form of cardiovascular exercise. That means it's good for your heart. According to the American Council on Exercise, walking has these major benefits:

- Lowers cholesterol
- Lowers blood pressure
- Increases energy and fitness
- Prevents weight gain

Guidelines for Stretching

- Don't stretch your muscles when they're cold. Walk at a light pace for 5 or 10 minutes before doing your warm-up stretch. Then stretch again after you exercise.

- Stretch all of your major muscle groups, not just your legs. Also, be sure to stretch both sides of your body.

- Don't bounce when you stretch. Instead, hold the stretch for about 30 seconds. Also repeat each stretch three or four times.

- Don't stretch to the point of hurting. You should feel tension, not pain.

- Add movement to your stretching. For instance, reach up or out with your arms while stretching your legs. Think of the movements used in yoga and the martial arts.

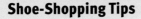

Shoe-Shopping Tips

1. Shop for shoes at the end of the day or after you've walked.
2. Wear or bring along the same socks you normally wear when you walk.
3. Try on both shoes. Many people's feet are not exactly the same size.
4. To get a feel for the shoes, walk around in the store for a few minutes on a hard surface.
5. After buying the shoes, try them out for a few days by wearing them around the house. Return them if you're not completely happy with them.
6. If possible, buy two pair of the same shoes, and alternate wearing them. Doing so will let the shoes air out between uses. It will also double your time between shoe purchases.

Walking Clubs

Check out your local community center or health club to find walking clubs in your area. Or find clubs by searching online for "walking clubs." Organizations such as the American Volkssport Association (VAA) hold events for walkers. They also offer guidelines on starting and running your own walking club.

CHAPTER **3**

Biking: The Rules of the Road

Wanda's Whirled of Wheels is a popular cycle shop. Wanda does more than sell bicycles, though. She also offers classes in bike maintenance and safety. She encourages cyclists to invest in safety equipment, such as helmets, lights, bright clothing, flags, and mirrors. With each purchase, Wanda's customers take home a printed sheet of rules of the road.

[FACT]

Helmet Laws

Twenty-one states and Washington, DC, have helmet laws for bicycle riders. However, most of these laws require only young riders (under age 16) to wear helmets. Some cities and counties have tougher laws, requiring all riders to wear helmets.

Being a Defensive Rider

Most guidelines for bicycle safety say to wear a helmet and to follow all traffic laws. But the fact is, you can follow both of these suggestions and still get hit by a car. Guidelines for defensive riding go beyond these basics. They teach you how to recognize dangerous situations and do your best to avoid them.

Rules of the Road for Cyclists

Follow these rules to make sure you have a safe and defensive riding style:

→ Know and obey all the local traffic rules.

→ Assume that motorists will not see you. Drivers expect to see other motorists and may not notice a cyclist.

[FACT]

Be Invisible!

One rule for defensive riding is "Ride as if you are invisible." This doesn't mean that you should try *not* to be seen. Instead, it means that you should assume drivers don't see you and then stay out of their way. For example, when riding on a busy street, stay as far to the  right as possible. Keep in mind that the more you rely on cars not to hit you, the more chance you take of being hit.

→ Don't keep your eyes on the roadway beneath you. Instead, scan the road ahead to anticipate problems or obstacles.

→ Ride only one person on a bicycle. (Only a special bike called a *tandem* is built for two people.)

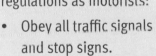

→ Ride on the right side of the road along with the traffic. In most places, it's illegal for a bicyclist to ride against the traffic or on the sidewalk.

→ Keep both hands on the handlebars. A busy stretch of road is not a good place to take a drink from your water bottle.

→ Use lights and wear bright or reflective clothing when riding at night.

[FACT]

Cyclists as Drivers

In most states, bicycle riders have the same rights and responsibilities as motor vehicle drivers. In addition, bike riders must follow the same laws and regulations as motorists:

- Obey all traffic signals and stop signs.
- Ride in the same direction as other traffic, not against it.
- Ride near the curb or edge of the roadway, not on the sidewalk. Ride in the center of the lane, with traffic, only if moving at the same speed as the other traffic.
- Move to the left to pass a parked or moving vehicle or to avoid a hazard.
- Signal every turn in advance, and turn from the correct lane.
- Stop at crosswalks to allow pedestrians to cross the street.
- Yield the right of way.

- Don't "hitch" a ride by holding onto another vehicle.

- Never ride a bike after using drugs or drinking alcohol.

- Be sure to signal before you turn.

- Ride in a straight line at a steady pace. This allows motorists to predict your course.

- Before entering a road or an intersection, look left, right, and left again.

- Make eye contact with drivers.

[FACT]

A Common Cycling Accident

One of the most common types of cycling accidents is called "dooring" or "getting doored." It involves a cyclist running into a car door that opens unexpectedly into the bike lane. The cyclist is injured  from hitting the door and being thrown off the bike. In some cases, cyclists are thrown into traffic and run over. "Dooring" accidents occur often on crowded city streets. To prevent dooring, drivers are encouraged to check their rear-view mirrors before opening their doors into the bike lane. And cyclists are encouraged to look for people sitting inside parked cars.

→ When riding next to parked cars, look through the rear windows. Watch for drivers pulling out or opening car doors.

→ Even though you have the right of way, don't take it for granted. Automobiles have much better protection in an accident than bikers do. Being right does not always mean being safe!

→ Some streets are just too dangerous to ride on, even with proper skills and defensive riding. Sometimes, it's best simply to avoid certain roads.

Biking to School or Work

Riding your bike to school or work has several benefits. It saves you money, gives you regular exercise, and is good for the environment. To make sure your commute is safe and trouble free, bring along the necessary equipment:

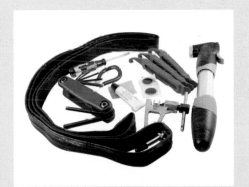

1. A bicycle that's properly sized and adjusted for you
2. A white light in front and a red reflector in the back (for night riding)
3. A carrying rack over the rear wheel
4. A basic tool kit, including tire-patching materials and a tire pump

CHAPTER **4**

Ride Sharing: Going My Way?

Do you hate driving in rush-hour traffic? Sometimes, the daily drive to school or work can seem like a job in itself. It can be costly, too! Sharing a ride may reduce your ***commuting*** woes. Options include carpools, ride shares, van pools, and car shares. They all provide a way to cut both your transportation costs and your frustrations.

Commuting

Traveling regularly between places, such as home and work or school.

The Cost of Commuting

How can you figure out how much you spend driving to work or school? Go online to a Web site such as TicketToRide.org, and use the carpool savings calculator. It will ask for information such as how far and how often you drive. It will also ask what gas mileage your car gets, how much gas costs per gallon, and how much you pay to park. Based on this information, the calculator will tell you how much it costs you to drive every year. And based on that, it will tell you how much you could save by carpooling.

Carpools

A *carpool* is formed when two or more people share a ride on a regular basis. Carpoolers may be friends, neighbors, or co-workers. Usually, they take turns driving their own vehicles.

These commuters cut expenses by sharing fuel costs and reducing wear and tear on their vehicles. Some Web sites have tools that will help you figure out the savings from carpooling. For more information, search online for the term "carpool savings." You may also find information about getting involved in carpooling at school or work.

Carpooling has other advantages, as well:

→ Carpoolers can drive in *HOV (High-Occupancy Vehicle) lanes*. The traffic in these lanes tends to flow faster.

→ Commuters often enjoy the company and conversation of their fellow riders. They find travel time less stressful.

→ Some insurance companies offer reduced rates for regular carpoolers.

→ Carpooling helps the environment, too. After all, fewer vehicles on the road mean less traffic and air pollution.

HOV (High-Occupancy Vehicle) lanes
Special lanes on highways that can be used only by vehicles with two or more passengers.

Reasons for Carpooling
A survey of carpoolers in Houston, Texas, asked them why they liked to share a ride. Here are their top five reasons:

1. Get to use HOV lanes
2. Relax while commuting
3. Save money on travel expenses
4. Enjoy traveling with others
5. Help the environment and society/Save time (tied)

Online Resources for Ride Sharing

Go online to get information about carpooling and other forms of ride sharing in your area. Check out these Web sites:

- CommuterPage.com
- eRideShare.com
- DivideTheRide.com
- RideshareOnline.com
- Craigslist (Rideshare listing)

Other Types of Ride Sharing

→ **Ride shares:** Some local and regional organizations set up ride shares. They match drivers and riders who can travel together. Trips can be scheduled on a regular or one-time basis for local travel or long-distance trips. To learn about local services, search for "ride share" on the Internet.

→ **Van pools:** Groups of 7 to 15 passengers can ride together in vans. Most people in van pools pay a set rate to travel a specific distance. For example, one pool offers a 20-mile daily ride for $60 a month. Regional van pools can be found online or in the phone book.

→ **Car sharing:** In big cities, owning a car can be difficult. For instance, where can you park? How can you manage the traffic? Car share organizations are perfect for many city dwellers. These organizations own a number of cars, which members can reserve for personal or business use. Members pay a fee to belong to the group. They also pay charges per hour or mile. These charges cover the shared costs of car payments, insurance, gas, and maintenance.

Car Sharing for College Students

Several car-sharing companies make vehicles available to college students. Students pay a low membership fee. Then, they can rent vehicles for hourly or daily rates. These rates usually cover use of the vehicle plus gas, insurance, maintenance, parking, and emergency services.

Being able to car share means that many college students won't bring their own cars to campus. This helps lessen the parking problems that exist at many colleges. Also, car-sharing companies are willing to rent vehicles to college students. Most rental car companies require drivers to be 25 or older.

Traveling by Bus

High gas prices and heavy traffic are two of the reasons many people decide to ride the bus. Riding the bus saves both time and money. That's especially true if you buy a monthly or yearly pass. Riding the bus is convenient, too, once you know how to use a route map and bus schedule. Find out for yourself why the bus is the most popular form of public transportation.

Why Not Ride the Bus?

Tani has found traveling her city by bus convenient and safe. A covered bus stop is located just one block from her apartment. A bus arrives there every 15 minutes, so Tani never has to wait very long. That bus line takes her directly downtown. There, at the main bus station, she can get on other buses. Those buses run on lines throughout the city.

Tani is seldom late for classes, work, or appointments. Why? She can predict exactly when she'll arrive at each destination by reading the bus schedule. Plus, she never has to worry about stopping to get gas or finding a place to park.

In the winter, when the roads are covered with ice and snow, Tani doesn't need to put chains on her tires. The public buses are chained and ready to go. In any kind of weather, buses generally have a better safety record than passenger cars.

In the summer, Tani enjoys riding her bicycle in a park on the edge of the city. Her bus line allows cyclists to load their bikes on a special rack on the front of each bus. Tani loads up her bike and gets dropped off at the park.

Tani's brother uses a wheelchair, and taking the bus works well for him, too. The Americans with Disabilities Act of 1990 requires public transportation systems to be accessible to disabled riders. In Tani's city, buses have lifts for people in wheelchairs and Braille signage for blind riders.

CHAPTER **1**

The Benefits of Public Transportation

The United States' first public bus service started in 1905. By 1914, New York City's motorized buses had completely replaced horse-drawn forms of transportation.

Mass transit

A public transportation system designed to move a large number of passengers within a city or region.

Today, buses are still the most common type of *mass transit* for city dwellers. But several other types of public transportation are available in many cities, too.

Mass Transit in the Horse-and-Buggy Days

In fact, public transportation in the United States dates back to the 1820s. Several horse-drawn forms of mass transit operated in New York City:

- Large stagecoaches called *omnibuses* ran regular routes. They were supposed to hold 15 passengers. But in many cases, more people squeezed inside and rode on top of coaches. The driver knew when to stop to let passengers off when someone pulled on a strap on his ankle.

- Another early form of public transportation was a streetcar pulled by a horse. These *horsecars* were pulled along a track sunk into the road. They held more people than omnibuses and provided a smoother ride. Passengers got the driver to stop by ringing a bell.

Horse-drawn forms of mass transit faced several problems. The horses were slow and had trouble climbing hills. Pulling the coaches was so hard that most horses worked only five years. And, of course, the horses left the city streets covered with manure.

Sadly, in 1872, an outbreak of the horse flu killed many of the animals used for public transportation in New York City. It also showed city leaders that they could not rely on one form of public transportation.

Types of Public Transportation

Most urban mass transit systems have a fleet of
buses. They travel regular routes, sharing the
streets with cars and trucks. And they run
on regular schedules, stopping at specific
locations at set times. In most large cities,
riders can get a *transfer* from one bus or
bus line to another. Doing so allows them to ride the
bus across the city and back.

Many cities also offer some type of train or rail
transportation. Subways and elevated rail lines carry passengers
on electrically powered trains. Subways run underground, whereas
elevated trains run aboveground. Both types of trains may have one or
several cars, and they may hold several hundred people.

Elevated trains and subways became popular in the mid- to late-
1800s. The fast growth of several US cities had made traffic a huge
problem on city streets. Transporting people above and below the
ground was a new idea. The first elevated train system in the United
States operated in New York in 1868. The first subway operated in
Boston in 1897.

Another type of railway is light rail transit (LRT). It also operates
using electricity. The power is usually provided by an overhead electrical line. LRTs often run on tracks in the middle of a street or beside

Transfer

A special ticket that allows changing from one bus or train to another.

38

[FACT]

Billions of Bus Rides

In 2010, Americans took 10.2 billion trips using the nation's public transportation systems. As shown below, 54% of public transportation is comprised of buses.

① Buses: **54%**
② Paratransit vehicles: **28%**
③ Rail systems: **12%**
④ Other modes: **6%**

a street. They may have one car or several cars and carry up to several hundred people per trip. LRT is seen as a clean, modern form of mass transit.

Over the years, LRT systems have replaced streetcars, trolleys, and trams in many cities. LRT first became popular in Germany and Great Britain after World War II. In North America, the Canadian city of Edmonton, Alberta, built the first LRT in 1978. And in 1981, San Diego, California, became the first US city to have light rail. Since then, many US cities have built LRT systems.

In rural areas and areas with low demand for public transportation, *DRT (Demand-Responsive Transit)* systems are sometimes available. DRTs have flexible schedules and routes. Also, the destination and departure points may change. A DRT is somewhat like a ride share but on a larger scale.

DRT (Demand-Responsive Transit)

A form of public transportation that uses small- to medium-sized vehicles, such as vans, to pick up and drop off passengers based on their needs.

Saving Time and Money

Buses cost less to operate and use less fuel than airplanes or trains, so *fares* are low. Some companies and schools even offer free or discounted bus *passes* to their employees. Also, people who ride the bus don't have to budget for parking, car insurance, gasoline, and maintenance.

Riding the bus allows commuters to make good use of their travel time. While riding, they can read, study, check e-mail, or send text messages.

People who don't ride buses enjoy the benefits of mass transit, too. Traffic congestion goes down when more commuters take the bus. And less traffic on the road means less pollution in the air.

These reasons explain why many cities encourage bus travel. Some even create special lanes to speed buses to their destinations. Other cities create downtown "fareless squares," where bus travel is free.

Fare
The fee paid to ride on a bus, train, or other form of public transportation.

Pass
A type of ticket that allows riding a bus for a certain number of trips or for a certain length of time.

CHAPTER 2

Using a Route Map

Brett lives on the corner of 4th Street and Oak Drive in a part of his city known as West Highlands. Each day, he takes city bus #43 from home to Highland Park High School and back again. When he wants to shop, he takes a convenient bus ride to the local mall. For trips to the city center, Brett transfers from bus #43 to the light rail train. The electric cars whisk him into the heart of town.

Brett plays shortstop for the Purple Hornets, a city league baseball team. His games are often held at Lakeside Park. To get there, he takes a short bus ride and another trip on the light rail. Some of Brett's teammates live in other parts of the city. They park their cars at the **Park & Ride** and meet up with Brett aboard bus #43.

Park & Ride

A parking lot where commuters leave their vehicles and board a form of public transportation, such as a bus or rail system. These lots are usually located in suburbs or on the edges of large cities.

Route Maps

Route maps, such as the one on the next page, help Brett and other passengers plan their bus trips. Notice the *legend* in the upper-left-hand corner. It explains the *symbols* on the map. For example, in the map for Route 43 West Highlands, an oval with an "S" inside it is the symbol for a scheduled bus stop. A rectangle with an "O" inside it symbolizes a light rail station.

As you study the map, see if you can find Brett's house. From there, trace the routes Brett travels on trips to school, the mall, the city center, and the park.

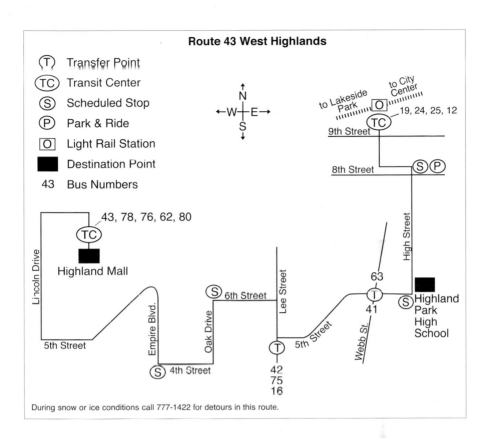

Route map

A map showing the route or routes traveled by one or more buses.

Legend

A list or chart identifying all of the symbols used on a map. It's sometimes called the *key*.

Symbols

On a map, the shapes, abbreviations, patterns, and colors used to represent features such as roadways, and buildings.

Complete Map Toolkit and Legend

HIGHWAY		GRASS FIELD	
MAJOR ROAD		SEA	
SECONDARY ROAD		FOREST	
RIVER		BUS STATION	
PROPOSED ROAD		TAXI STAND	
BRIDGE		LIGHT RAIL STATION	
TOLL		TRAIN STATION	
TRAFFIC LIGHT		AIRPORT	
ONE WAY		SEAPORT	
HOUSING WITH NUMBER BESIDE ROAD		APARTMENT	
LIGHT RAIL & STATION		FACTORY	
TRAIN RAIL & STATION		MUSEUM	
STATE BOUNDARY		CHURCH	
CITY BOUNDARY			

CHINESE TEMPLE		INFORMATION KIOSK	
MOSQUE		COURTHOUSE	
HINDU TEMPLE		PARKING AREA	
SCHOOL		SWIMMING POOL	
COMMUNITY HALL		FAST FOOD	
POLICE STATION		FOOD COURT	
FIRE STATION		CINEMA	
HOSPITAL		PUBLIC TOILET	
LIBRARY		TELEPHONE	
POST OFFICE		GAS STATION	
EMBASSY		RESTING AREA	
SHOPPING MALL		GOLF COURSE	
HOTEL		PLAYGROUND	
PLACE OF INTEREST		NUCLEAR REACTOR	

CHAPTER **3**

A Bus Schedule

All *transit companies* publish *schedules* to help riders plan their travels. Free printed copies are usually available in public places, such as post offices, libraries, shopping centers, and banks.

Transit companies

Businesses that operate mass transit or public transportation, such as bus companies.

Schedule

For public transportation, a list of departure and arrival times organized by location. It's sometimes called a *timetable*.

48

In many cities, bus riders can call in and hear a recorded schedule over the telephone. Riders can usually find schedule information online, too.

In Chapter 2, you met Brett, a regular bus rider. He keeps the schedule handy for bus line #43. Take a look at the weekday schedule, which is shown on the following page.

Reading a Bus Schedule

A bus schedule is fairly easy to read. You just need to understand what information is provided in what places:

→ Read from top to bottom to find out the departure times at each scheduled stop.

→ Read from left to right to figure how long it takes to get from point to point along the route.

→ The numbers listed immediately under the stop points show the numbers of transfer bus lines.

BUS SCHEDULE

#43 WEST HIGHLANDS

Weekdays → To City Center

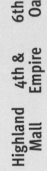

Highland Mall	4th & Empire	6th & Oak	5th & Lee	5th & Webb	5th & High	8th & High	9th & High
43, 78, 76, 62, 80			42, 75, 16	63, 41			19, 24, 25, 12
6:49	6:57	7:02	7:09	7:14	7:19	7:25	7:30
7:49	7:57	8:02	8:09	8:14	8:19	8:25	8:30
8:49	8:57	9:02	9:09	9:14	9:19	9:25	9:30
9:46	9:55	10:01	10:08	10:14	10:19	10:25	10:30
10:46	10:55	11:01	11:08	11:14	11:19	11:25	11:30

① Route number and area of city

② Days schedule applies to and final destination of route

③ Locations of scheduled bus stops

④ Numbers of transfer bus lines available at these stops

11:46	11:55	12:01	12:08	12:14	12:19	12:25	12:30
12:46	12:55	1:01	1:08	1:14	1:19	1:25	1:30
1:46	1:55	2:01	2:08	2:14	2:19	2:25	2:30
2:46	2:55	3:01	3:08	3:14	3:19	3:25	3:30
3:46	3:55	4:01	4:08	4:14	4:19	4:25	4:30
4:46	4:55	5:01	5:08	5:14	5:19	5:25	5:30
5:46	5:55	6:01	6:08	6:14	6:19	6:25	6:30
6:46	6:55	7:01	7:08	7:14	7:19	7:25	7:30
7:46	7:55	8:01	8:08	8:14	8:19	8:25	8:30

⑤ Times of scheduled stops

⑥ Notes with additional details

- Light figures are a.m. hours. **Dark figures** are **p.m.** hours.
- Use a Weekend Schedule for Saturdays, Sundays, and Holidays. Holidays include New Year's Day, Memorial Day, Independence Day, Labor Day, Thanksgiving, and Christmas Day.
- Schedule times MAY BE CHANGED by as much as three minutes to relieve overcrowding or adjust to traffic conditions.
- For Braille, large print, or audio schedules, call 777-1179 or visit our Web site.

51

Types of Bus Lines

City Bus Lines

People like Brett ride buses in cities and towns all over the United States. In the nation's biggest cities, buses often run 24 hours a day and routes go to most neighborhoods. Bus service to areas beyond the city usually runs during the day and into the evening. Late-night service is limited, however. Small cities often have bus lines but offer many fewer routes.

New York City has the nation's largest city bus line. The Metropolitan Transportation Authority, or MTA, carries 2.5 million riders a day.

Regional Bus Lines

In addition to city bus lines, many regional bus lines carry Americans on a daily basis. About 70 **interstate** bus lines operate across the United States.

One example is Peter Pan Bus Lines, which connects cities and towns throughout the Northeast. The company began service in 1933 with a route that ran from Northhampton to Boston, Massachusetts. Routes were added as highways made traveling by bus fast and economical. Today, Peter Pan buses travel 25 million miles a year. And its modern coaches are equipped with Internet service, electrical outlets for charging telephones, and *GPS*.

National Bus Lines

Several bus lines provide service nationwide. The largest is Greyhound Lines. It began service in 1914 in a small town in northern Minnesota. A bus brought miners to and from the area's ore mines. Service soon spread across Minnesota and Wisconsin and into Canada. Today, Greyhound provides service to more than 2,300 cities across the United States, Canada, and Mexico. The company's buses make about 13,000 trips a day, and in a year, they carry 25 million passengers. Luxury coaches have leather seats, increased legroom, Internet service, and electrical outlets.

Interstate
Occurring between states.

GPS (Global Positioning System)
A computerized navigation system that uses a network of satellites to show the position of a vehicle, ship, or person.

CHAPTER 4
Easy, Economical Rides

Riding a city bus can be an inexpensive way to get around. *Thrifty* riders can get even more for their money by taking advantage of special fares. Look for the best values on the chart below.

Thrifty
Careful with money; economical.

Fares	Cash	10-Ticket Book	Monthly Pass	Annual Pass
All-City	$2.00	$18.75	$72	$650
Youth (ages 7–15)	$1.00	$9.25	$36	$325
Honored Citizen (age 65+)	$0.75	$7.00	$27	$250
Special Fares		Cost		
Quick Tik (valid for 6 hrs.)		$3.00		
All-Day Ticket		$5.00		
School Pass (elementary, middle, or high school students; for weekday use)		$20.00/month		
Adventure Pass (3 days)		$14.00		

- Exact change is needed for cash fares
- Up to 3 children age 6 and under ride free with a paying passenger.

CITY TRANSIT AUTHORITY

Tickets versus Passes

Keep in mind that a *ticket* is usually good for a single ride. However, a *pass* is usually good for multiple rides over a certain period of time. For example, if you have an annual pass, you can ride as many times as you want—not just once a day. Also, the driver will usually take your ticket. But he or she will just want to see your pass. You keep the pass and reuse it for the time period it covers.

Buying Bus Tickets and Passes

Tickets and passes can usually be purchased at transit company offices and outlets. They may also be for sale by mail or online. Some employers and schools offer *discounted* passes or tickets. Make sure to ask.

Discounted

Reduced in price; inexpensive.

[FACT]

Bus Passes at Universities

Many universities offer students bus passes at discounted prices. For example, students at the University of Minnesota can get what's called a U-Pass. That pass allows them to ride Minneapolis buses and light rail trains 24 hours a day, 7 days a week. The U-Pass costs $97 a semester. That's an estimated savings of 71% over the cost of regular bus fares.

Tips for Riding the Bus

Before boarding your city bus, check out these tips for successful riding:

→ Be at the bus stop a few minutes before the bus is scheduled to arrive.

→ Look for the sign "Bus Stop" to make sure you're waiting in the right place.

→ Wave as the bus nears, so the driver will know to stop.

→ Respect *priority* seating areas for seniors and passengers with disabilities.

Priority
Considered of greatest importance or being of main concern.

→ When you board, place the exact fare or ticket in the fare box or show your pass.

→ Keep the transfer ticket the driver hands you, and use it to switch from bus to bus. Check the time noted on the transfer to see when it expires.

→ Let the driver know your stop is coming up. Use one of the pull cords, signal strips, or signal buttons.

→ Before you get off the bus, check to make sure you have all your personal items.

→ In case of an emergency, notify the driver.

After Leaving the Bus

After you've stepped off the bus, wait until it pulls away before crossing the street. And then, cross at the nearest crosswalk and at the correct time. Never cross the street in front of the bus. Remember that other vehicles don't have to stop for passengers exiting a city bus, like they do for children exiting a school bus. Also, don't cross behind the bus and walk into traffic. Other drivers may not see you in time to stop.

SECTION 3

Traveling by Train or Plane

Traveling by train versus plane provides two very different experiences. Train travel is slow paced and relaxed. It also lets you see the sights along the way. Air travel is faster and can take you to more places. Today, flights can take you all over the world. When planning your next trip, be sure to consider what each type of travel has to offer.

It's Vacation Time!

Liam had finally earned some vacation time at his job. And he knew exactly where he wanted to go: Chicago. His brother had moved there last year and kept asking him to visit. He talked about going to ballgames, visiting museums, going to comedy clubs, and more.

Liam had never been far from Seattle, his hometown. He was interested in seeing the country between there and Chicago. Driving was out of the question, because it would take too long. Liam only had one week of vacation. So he thought about two other options: taking the train and flying.

Liam chose the dates for his trip. Then he started to look into the two kinds of travel. He found a lot of information online about schedules and costs. He was surprised to learn that flying and taking the train cost about the same. But there was a huge difference in the

time needed for travel. To fly to Chicago would take almost 6 hours each way. But to take the train would take almost 2 days each way.

Liam thought seriously about taking the train. He had never traveled by rail and really wanted to see the sights along the way. But he just couldn't take up 4 days of his vacation traveling. In the end, he decided to fly and to spend the extra time with his brother.

CHAPTER 1

The Benefits of Traveling by Train

"All aboard!"

Hearing these words, rail passengers climb onboard a train and begin their travels. For many people, a train ride is more than just a way of getting from place to place. The trip is an experience. It's time

to sit back, relax, and enjoy the passing scenery and city skylines. Some trains offer a two-level **sightseeing** car that gives passengers a widespread view of the sights.

Comfort and Convenience

Train travel can be comfortable and convenient. Riders can relax in their seats, or they can get up and wander or stretch their legs at any time. Riders on some trains even spend the night onboard. Many overnight trains offer sleeping **berths or compartments.** (There is an extra charge for these, however.)

Many overnight trains also have a **full-service** dining car. Trains that travel shorter routes often have snack bars.

Sightseeing
Visiting tourist attractions and other places of interest.

Berths or compartments
Private places to sit or sleep.

Full-Service
Containing a complete range of foods and beverages and service by waiters and waitresses.

Speed

In a hurry? On a short trip, a train can actually get you to your destination faster than a car or plane. Also, train passengers don't need to worry about traffic or finding rest stops.

Because many airports are located just outside big cities, they're difficult to reach. The ride to the airport and the lines through check-in and security can add to travel time. On the other hand, many train stations are conveniently located in city centers. And check-in is usually quick.

Amtrak

Amtrak is the company that controls passenger rail travel between US cities. Amtrak was created by the US government in 1971. Today, it serves more than 500 cities in 46 states.

To increase ticket sales, Amtrak offers some bargain fares. Special rail passes allow unlimited travel within certain boundaries and certain time periods. Amtrak also offers fare discounts for children, people with disabilities, students, military personnel, veterans, and seniors over 62. Many Americans find the train the most practical, economical, and scenic way to travel.

[FACT]

Discounts and Deals on Amtrak

Amtrak's Web site says that it offers "everyday discounts, limited-time specials and unique passes and travel programs." Here are some examples:

- USA Rail Passes are available for 15-, 30-, and 45-day travel across the United States.

- Multi-Ride Tickets can be purchased as monthly or 10-ride tickets. Another option offers college students six rides a year between certain cities.

- Tour packages take travelers to places such as Yosemite National Park and Sequoia National Park in California.

- Complete vacations provide rail travel plus hotels, meals, car rentals, and more.

  For special deals, check Amtrak's Web site at www.amtrak.com.

High-Speed Trains

For many years, Europe and Japan have used high-speed trains. Now, the United States is trying to catch up.

Acela is a good example. Run by Amtrak, its name suggests "acceleration" and "excellence." This high-tech, high-speed train connects Boston, New York, Philadelphia, Baltimore, and Washington, DC. It zooms passengers from city to city at speeds up to 150 miles per hour.

In 2009, the US Congress *allocated* $8 billion for rail projects. Priority was given to projects that promote high-speed rail development.

> **Allocated**
> Assigned or set to be given out.

[FACT]

The World's Fastest Trains

- Japan created the world's first high-speed train. It was built for the 1964 Olympics and carried passengers between Tokyo and Osaka. Today, so-called bullet trains travel at speeds up to 185 miles per hour. Approximately 1,500 miles of rail lines criss-cross Japan.

- Europe's first high-speed train was built in Italy. It opened in 1978 and ran between Rome and Florence. Now, Spain, Germany, Belgium, Great Britain, and France all have trains that travel at speeds of 150 miles per hour or more.

- Taiwan and China have created the world's fastest trains to date. The train that runs from Beijing to Tianjin reaches 217 miles per hour. This 75-mile route was completed for the 2008 Olympics. And the train that runs between the city of Shanghai and its airport travels at 268 miles per hour.

CHAPTER **2**

Buying Airline Tickets

When Liam starting planning his trip to Chicago, he knew that airfare would eat up much of his budget. He was hoping to get a low fare. But when he

> **Book**
>
> To reserve or arrange.

went on WXYZ Airlines' Web site to **book** his flight, he realized he had many questions:

→ Did he want a nonstop or a direct flight?

→ Could he book in advance?

→ Should he fly first class, business class, or coach?

→ Could he travel midweek or only on the weekends?

Liam also saw that there were many kinds of fares: Excursion fares, Super Savers, Super-Duper Savers, Max Savers, Penny Pinchers, and Dollar-Stretchers. He soon realized that he needed to learn more about all these choices.

Liam decided to do some homework before booking his flight. He found that special deals, travel times, and ticket *restrictions* make a huge difference in costs. He also learned that full-fare tickets have few restrictions but come at the highest prices. Discount fares are for travelers who can meet certain *conditions.* These fares are the low-cost tickets advertised in newspapers and online. They may be less than half the cost of full-fare tickets.

Restrictions

Limitations created by rules or regulations.

Conditions

Circumstances or qualities.

Understanding Airline Terminology

Before you call a ***travel agent*** or airline or log onto the Internet to book a flight, here are some of the terms you should know:

→ **Coach/Economy class:** Most flyers go coach or economy, because it's the only class offering bargain prices. Passengers accept less leg room and service in exchange for cheaper tickets.

Travel agent

Someone who arranges all the details of a trip for a traveler, including the transportation, hotels, and schedule. This individual usually works in a business called a *travel agency.*

→ **First class:** The front of the plane usually has a first-class section. First-class travel is costly, but it does provide deluxe seating and fine food service.

→ **Business class:** Business-class tickets cost more than coach but less than first class. Offered by some airlines, they provide more comfortable seats and better service.

→ **Advance purchase requirement:** To get the best price, you must usually book your travel 14 or 21 days ahead for ***domestic*** flights and 30 days for ***international*** flights.

→ **Direct flight:** The plane will make one or more stops, but you won't change planes.

→ **Nonstop flight:** You will fly all the way from your departure point to your destination without stopping at another airport.

Domestic
A flight that begins and ends in the same country.

International
A flight that begins in one country and ends in another.

- → **Round trip:** A ticket that covers travel from one place to another and then back again.

- → **One way:** A ticket that covers travel from one place to another.

- → **Midweek departure:** A restriction that limits travel to Tuesday through Thursday.

- → **Length of stay:** With a discount, you must usually stay at least 3 days but not longer than 30 days.

- → **Saturday night stay:** You must remain at your destination over at least one Saturday night.

- → **Nonrefundable:** If you cancel, you won't get your money back. However, for a service fee, you can exchange most discount tickets.

- → **Excursion:** This is the lowest fare that major airlines offer. Look for these fares under other names, such as "Super Saver."

CHAPTER 3

Reading a Flight Itinerary

When you purchase an airline ticket, you'll receive an e-mailed or printed summary of your purchase and flight schedule. Angela purchased an airline ticket from her hometown of Phoenix, Arizona, to Oakland, California. She received the ***receipt and itinerary*** on the next page.

Receipt and Itinerary

A *receipt* is a printed statement showing that a specific payment has been made. An *itinerary* is a travel schedule, which includes details about the dates, times, and routes. When you purchase an airline ticket, the itinerary you receive may also serve as your receipt.

WXYZ AIRWAYS

Receipt and Itinerary

Bring a copy of this itinerary with you to the airport for flight check-in.

WXYZ Airways Confirmation Number: F7TCLV ①

Passenger(s): Angela T. Ramos

TRIP ITINERARY ②

Date	Day	Stops	Flight	Routing
Jul 19	Fri	N/S	1101	Depart Phoenix (PHX) 6:20 a.m., arrive Oakland (OAK) 8:10 a.m. ③
Jul 22	Mon	N/S	1870	Depart Oakland (OAK) 2:10 p.m., arrive Phoenix (PHX) 5:00 p.m.

Type of Fare	Base Fare	Taxes	Passenger(s)	Total	Fare Code
Discount Fare PHX-OAK-PHX	$200.00	$21.00	1	$221.00	QE7NR ④

BILLING INFORMATION

Credit Card Holder: Angela T. Ramos
Billing Address: 1421 Adobe Ave.
Phoenix, AZ 99210
Form of Payment: City Charge xxxxxxxxxxxxxxxx

For questions concerning your flight, call WXYZ Airways at 1-800-FLYWXYZ (1-800-359-9999), or visit our Web site at www.flywxyz.com.

① Confirmation Number

A confirmation number is assigned to the traveler when he or she purchases a ticket. It is the traveler's proof or evidence of having made the purchase. Angela will refer to this number if she has questions about her flight.

② Trip Itinerary Information

This section provides several important details about the itinerary. The top row of information provides details about the departure flight. Reading across, from left to right, Angela can see that she is leaving home on July 19, which is a Friday. She is on a nonstop flight, as shown by the N/S. The flight number is 1101. Finally, the flight leaves Phoenix at 6:20 a.m. and arrives at Oakland at 8:10 a.m. The second row of information provides the same kinds of details about her return flight. The bottom row provides information about the fare Angela paid for her round-trip flight.

❸ Airport Codes

Most airports around the world are identified by a unique three-letter code. For example, on Angela's itinerary, the Phoenix airport is identified with the code PHX and the Oakland airport with the code OAK. These codes are assigned by the International Air Transport Association (IATA). They are referred to as IATA location identifiers. The coding system was designed to make it easier for pilots, air traffic controllers, baggage handlers, and others to refer to specific airports. Some of the codes are obvious, such as those for Phoenix and Oakland. But others are harder to figure out, such as ORD for O'Hare International Airport in Chicago, Illinois.

❹ Fare Codes

Fare codes give information about the type of booking. The fare code on Angela's itinerary is QE7NR. It means 7-day advance purchase, round trip, valid all days, Saturday-night stay, and nonrefundable.

Be on Time!

- **For a domestic flight:**
Arrive at the airport 90 minutes before your scheduled departure time. Most airlines require that you be checked in 30 to 45 minutes before your scheduled departure time.
But some airports require a longer time, especially if you are checking baggage. Most airlines also require that you be at the gate at least 15 minutes before the scheduled departure time.

- **For an international flight:** Arrive at the airport 3 hours before your scheduled departure time. Most airlines require that you be checked in 60 to 90 minutes before your scheduled departure time. This is true whether or not you are checking baggage. Most airlines also require that you be at the gate at least 30 minutes before the scheduled departure time.

Check-In Requirements

Be sure to give yourself plenty of time before your flight. After you arrive at the airport, you'll need time to complete all ticketing, baggage check, and

Procedures
Methods or processes.

security *procedures* and arrive at the gate ready to board.

Check your travel itinerary to find out the airline's check-in requirements. Here's what Angela's itinerary said:

You must be checked in at least 30 minutes before your scheduled departure time. You must be at the gate at least 15 minutes before your scheduled departure time. Failure to meet these check-in requirements may result in you missing your flight and paying fees to change your ticket.

Changing Your Itinerary

Also check your itinerary for the airline's **policy** about changing flights. For instance, what if you want to fly at a different time or on a different

Policy

Rule or plan.

day? Or what if you want to cancel the trip entirely?

Most airlines will charge a fee to change your itinerary. The usual charge is $50 or more. If you cancel your trip, the airline won't likely refund your money. But it may give you what's called a *travel voucher*. That voucher will let you exchange your ticket for another one of the same value.

Here's what Angela's itinerary said about making changes:

Any change to this itinerary may result in a fare increase. Unless otherwise noted, if you do not travel on this itinerary, you may qualify for an exchange or refund. To apply for a refund, call WXYZ Airways at 1-800-FLYWXYZ or visit our Web site at www.flywxyz.com.

CHAPTER **4**

Overseas Travel

What Is a Passport?

You'll need a passport to travel outside the United States. A passport is an official document that *certifies* your identity and citizenship.

> **Certify**
> To confirm or prove that something is true or correct.

Having a passport means you're allowed to travel outside your country.

Passports are issued by national governments to their citizens. If you are an American, your passport will be issued by the US Department of State. It will identify you as a US citizen. You will show your passport when you enter and leave most countries and when you return home.

[FACT]

Demand for Passports

Since June 1, 2009, Americans have been required to have a passport to return to the United States from almost any foreign country. This requirement applies whether travel is by land, sea, or air. In the past, Americans could travel by land to other countries without a passport. Now, when traveling to Canada or Mexico Americans must use a passport.

Because passports are now required for any travel outside the US, the demand for getting them has increased a lot. In 2005, the US Department of State issued 10.1 million passports. And in 2007, it issued a record high 18.4 million. An estimated 15 million passports were issued in 2010.

How Can You Get a Passport?

Follow these steps to get a passport:

1. **Fill out a form.** Pick up an application form at the post office, courthouse, or passport agency office, or find the form online. If you have never had a passport or are a minor (under 18 years old), you must turn in the form in person. *Expired* passports can be renewed by mail.

2. **Prove that you're a citizen.** If you were born in the United States, a certified copy of your birth certificate is required

> **Expire**
> To come to an end and no longer be useful or valid.

   to prove your citizenship. If you became a US citizen, you must present your certificate of naturalization.

3. **Get your picture taken.** You will need two identical color photographs that show a front view of your face. They must be 2 inches by 2 inches in size.

4. **Prove who you are.** Acceptable forms of identification may include a driver's license or military ID.

5. **Pay the fee.** If you're under 16, the fee to get a passport is $80. If you're 16 or over, the fee is $110. First-time applicants also must pay a special $25 fee, called an *execution fee.*

The US Department of State suggests allowing 4 to 6 weeks to receive your passport. The months of March through September are usually the busiest times. You can also pay an extra $60 to have your

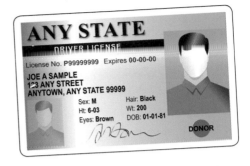

passport *expedited*, or processed more quickly. Getting an expedited passport usually takes 2 to 3 weeks.

Some countries require a **visa.** They also want to know your travel

plans before allowing you to enter. Their embassies in the United States can tell you if a visa is required.

Once you have your passport, it's good for only a certain number of years. For an adult, a passport is good for 10 years. For someone under age 18, a passport is good for 5 years. The expiration date will be printed on the passport.

Visa

A document that allows someone with a passport to enter a country for a specific purpose and time period.

Immunizations

Medical treatments that provide protection from certain diseases. The treatments usually involve injections using a needle. They are also called *vaccinations* or *shots*.

Traveling Overseas

Health and safety are important issues for travelers, especially when visiting overseas. Make sure that you bring along your medications and get all the suggested ***immunizations.*** You should also bring along information about your medical history, medications, and blood type, plus your doctor's name and phone number.

Before you travel, also find out about any travel warnings or travel alerts for the region you plan to visit. Contact the US Department of State to see whether it recommends avoiding a possibly dangerous area.

You can get more travel advice by reading travel guides, phoning specific agencies, or checking out Internet travel sites.

[FACT]

Travel Warnings and Travel Alerts

Before you travel overseas, go to the Web site of the US Department of State (http://travel.state.gov). Look for travel warnings and travel alerts about the country you plan to visit:

- **Travel warnings** recommend avoiding travel to certain countries. These warnings are issued for two main reasons. One reason is that ongoing conditions make a country dangerous or unstable. The second reason is that the US government cannot assist Americans in a country. This may occur because the US embassy has been closed or had its staff reduced.

- **Travel alerts** provide information about short-term conditions that may create risk. Examples include natural disasters, terrorist activities, and political demonstrations.

Planning a Vacation

If you could vacation anywhere in the world, where would you go? Why? You might someday be able to take that trip if you learn how to plan a vacation. Basic planning involves choosing a destination, setting a budget, and deciding how to get there and where to stay. Careful planning will help make sure all of your vacations are full of fun—not unwanted surprises!

Going Out on Her Own

Growing up, Carin had taken plenty of vacations with her family. They were always on a budget, it seemed. But they went a lot of places and had a lot of fun.

Now, Carin was thinking about taking a trip on her own. She couldn't afford to go very far or for very long. So she decided to take a weekend getaway.

Carin bought a guidebook about one of the states next to hers. Looking through it, she found three or four places she wanted to visit. Each was within several hours' drive of her home. After choosing one of the destinations, Carin went online. She got a lot of useful information

from the area's tourism bureau. She found out what she could do and where she could stay.

Gathering all this information also helped Carin plan her budget. She knew the exact distance to her destination. That helped her figure out what she'd have to spend on gas. She had also read about a historical hotel in the area. It was more expensive than some of the other hotels. But she really wanted to stay there! She planned to save money on other things, like eating out.

When the weekend of Carin's trip came along, she was more than ready to go. And because of her careful planning, the trip was a complete success. She could hardly wait to go again!

CHAPTER **1**

Selecting a Travel Destination

Choosing a vacation spot is different from choosing a new bike or outfit. You can't take a vacation spot for a test drive or try it on before making your decision. But you can find good *resources* to help you check out your destination before you leave home.

Resources

Things that provide information or advice about a particular topic.

Guidebooks

Guidebooks are loaded with valuable information. One travel writer describes them as "$25 tools for $4,000 experiences." Guidebooks give advice about sights to see and where to stay, eat, and shop. They provide weather statistics and hints on what clothes to pack. Most guidebooks contain maps, visa and immunization requirements, event schedules, and tour and transportation information. They are also convenient to use, because you can take them with you on your trip.

Many guidebooks are aimed at specific audiences. What does Backpacker Ben check out before he grabs his duffel bag and hits the road? He uses a guidebook aimed at adventurous, hardy, budget-minded travelers. But History-Buff Heidi chooses a guidebook packed with regional descriptions and details about art and culture.

Some guidebooks specialize in information about little-known points of interest. Others feature colorful pictures and helpful hints about nightlife and music. To choose the right guidebook, first think about your specific interests in a vacation destination.

Tips for Choosing a Guidebook

Before you buy a guide-book, study it. Ask these questions:

- How old is the guidebook? Has the information been updated in the last year or two?

- Who wrote the book? What is the author's experience?

- What kind of traveler is the book written for? Is it aimed at someone like you?

- Is the book interesting and readable? Do you get a sense of the place from reading about it?

- Does the book make a lot of strong recommendations? Does the author seem biased?

- Does the book contain too much information? Will you be able to use what's there?

Media Resources

Make sure to use your computer to explore travel ideas, too. Destination Web sites and online travel guides—even travel review Web sites—offer up-to-the-minute tips, photos, coupons, maps, answers to questions, and accounts of travelers' personal experiences. They may even have the most recent information about new, closed, or off-limits *locales* that guidebooks don't have in even their most current printing.

Locales

Locations or settings.

Travel Blogs

Many travelers write blogs about their experiences. Reading them may help you learn about a destination you're interested in. Check out these sites:

- www.everything-everywhere.com
- www.gadling.com
- www.travelblogs.com
- www.travelblog.org
- www.upgradetravelbetter.com

Your television can be another travel resource. The Discovery Channel can acquaint you with many interesting locales. Also check out the Travel Channel and the National Geographic channel, where armchair tourists can explore the world through viewing a range of programs.

Tourism Bureaus

Did you know that most countries, states, and cities have tourism bureaus? They will happily send you brochures that include details about scenery, attractions, lodging, and events. You may also find much of this information online.

Most hotels and resorts also send out brochures. Remember, however, that these are advertisements aimed at selling you on a certain destination.

Tourism Bureaus

Tourism bureaus pride themselves on providing information that's free, accurate, and unbiased. They don't promote specific hotels, restaurants, or airlines. To find a tourism

office for a destination that interests you, check out the Tourism Offices Worldwide Directory (www.towd.com). This Web site provides access to tourism bureaus for all 50 states and about 200 countries.

When to Go

Local celebrations, art shows, sporting events, and music festivals can be very entertaining. But be aware that a few drawbacks come along with the fun. Major events are usually crowded. That means that hotels will be hard to book, restaurants will have long lines, and traffic will be congested. Perhaps most importantly, prices will be at their peak.

Most popular travel destinations have high and low seasons. During the low season, prices are cheaper, places are less crowded, and the local people may even be more friendly.

Tips for Traveling in the Low Season

1. Contact the tourism bureau of a particular place to find out when the low season is. Also ask why it's the low season.

2. Weather is the number-one reason many places have a low season. Do some research to learn what the weather is like at this time.

3. Find out whether museums and other attractions are open normal hours during the low season.

4. Check out hotels. Find out whether all their services will be available during the low season. Also ask whether repairs or other work will be done during this time.

5. Check travel Web sites and talk to travel agents to find special deals for low-season travel.

CHAPTER 2

Planning Your Travel Budget

On your last vacation, how much money did you spend a day, on average?

That's the question the American Automobile Association (AAA) asked people in a nationwide survey. The AAA has been tracking vacation costs since 1950. Many Americans use this information to plan a vacation *budget*.

According to the AAA survey, two adults vacationing together spend an average of $244 a day. That cost covers *lodging* and meals. The average cost of lodging is $164 a day. And the average cost of meals is $80 a day, not including tips and beverages.

Of course, the other big cost of traveling is transportation. Flying is the most expensive way to get somewhere. Driving your own car is the least expensive. But as mentioned earlier, driving isn't an option in many cases.

> **Budgot**
>
> A plan for spending money. The plan is usually for a certain time period or a purchase.
>
> **Lodging**
>
> A place to stay, such as a hotel, bed-and-breakfast, or inn.

Where You Go

Travel costs vary widely by region. The most expensive place to vacation in the United States is Honolulu, Hawaii. There, the average daily cost of lodging and meals for two adults is $673. Here are some other expensive destinations:

→ New York City: $606 a day

→ San Diego, California: $361 a day

→ Miami, Florida: $370 a day

→ Las Vegas, Nevada: $358 a day

Kate and Jasmine's Travel Budget

Kate and Jasmine are traveling to Santa Fe, New Mexico. They are carefully planning a budget for their week's vacation. Take a look.

The least expensive places to vacation are Tulsa, Oklahoma, and Albuquerque, New Mexico. In both cities, the average daily cost of lodging and meals for two adults is $179. Other inexpensive destinations include the following:

→ Wichita, Kansas: $194 a day

→ Oklahoma City, Oklahoma: $194 a day

→ Fresno, California: $207 a day

Shuttle bus

A bus that takes people back and forth between two specific places. Shuttle buses often run between an airport and a hotel, for instance.

Splurge

To spend money freely or excessively.

Souvenir

Something that's bought or kept as a reminder of a person, place, or time.

Our Vacation Budget

Airfare: $350 round trip (to Albuquerque, closest major airport)

Hints: Book at least 14 days in advance, and stay over a Saturday night.

Taxi from Albuquerque Airport: $30 each way

Hint: The hotel shuttle bus is $10 each way.

Lodging: $75 (per person) per night (including tax)

Hints: Split the cost of a room, so we can afford a nice hotel. Budget for taxes and fees that will be added to the room rate. Low-season rates are 20 percent less.

Food: $30 to $40 per day

Hints: Hotels may include breakfast in their rate. Make lunch our major meal out, since dinner prices are higher. Remember to figure in tips. Limit snacks and treats at tourist spots. Get takeout food for dinner.

Recreation and entertainment: $25 per day average

Hints: Some days, we can entertain ourselves without spending a dime. But other days, we may splurge on a bike rental. Look for free fun, such as public concerts and free admission days at museums.

Shopping and souvenirs: $100 total

Hint: Look for local art fairs to buy souvenirs of Southwest art and culture.

Traveling with a Friend

→ Discuss what you're packing and agree in advance on what kinds of things you'll do. Will you take formal wear? Hiking boots?

→ Talk about sleep habits, TV viewing, air conditioning, and other personal preferences.

→ Plan to spend some time alone. One of you might shop while the other visits a museum, for example.

→ Talk about dining together. What kind of restaurants do you want to go to? Expensive? Budget? Agree to each pay your share of the bill. Split *miscellaneous* costs, such as cab fares.

Miscellaneous
Of different types or from different sources.

Tips for Reducing Travel Expenses

→ Look for free or low-cost locations and activities, such as public parks and concerts.

→ Avoid taking taxis. Walk, ride shuttle buses, and take public transportation.

→ Take advantage of the free breakfast offered at many hotels.

→ Carry your suitcase onboard the airplane instead of paying to check it.

→ Stay at a hotel just outside a downtown area or a short distance from a popular attraction.

→ If possible, fix some of your own meals or bring along prepared foods.

High Hotel Taxes and Fees

Often, hotels in big cities charge a number of extra taxes and fees. And in many cases, these extra charges add approximately 15% to the regular room rate. For example, in San Francisco, taxes and fees add $30 to a $200-a-night hotel room. In New York City, taxes and fees add $33 to a same-priced hotel room.

CHAPTER **3**

Fly or Drive?

Most people only consider flying to get to their destination. Their main goal is to get there as fast as possible. If that's your main goal and "Time is money," then flying might be your best choice.

But you might enjoy taking a road trip if you have plenty of time, a *reliable* car, and passengers to share the expenses. Traveling by car can be an economical and carefree way to travel.

Reliable
Dependable and consistent.

Which option is right for you? See pages 106–107 for a comparison of some of the costs, conveniences, and benefits of car travel versus air travel.

Top-Five US Driving Trips

1. Yosemite National Park and Beyond
From Oakhurst to Mono Lake, California (180 miles)
Enjoy the rustic beauty of Yosemite, the Sierra National Forest, the Tioga Pass, and other natural wonders.
Best time to go: spring or fall

2. Northeastern Arizona
From Tuba City to Canyon de Chelly (215 miles)
This drive features the deserts and canyons of the US Southwest. Also learn about the Native American Hopi and Navajo cultures.
Best time to go: winter or spring

3. Florida's Overseas Highway
From Florida City to Key West (127 miles)
Drive across 42 bridges of different lengths as you go from key to key. (*Keys* are small islands.) Key West is the southernmost point of the continental United States.
Best time to go: winter or spring

4. The Elvis Trail
From Nashville to Memphis, Tennessee (210 miles)
Start at the hometown of country western music and end up at the birthplace of Elvis Presley. Also learn about the struggle for equality in the United States at the National Civil Rights Museum in Memphis.
Best time to go: spring or summer

5. Vermont Ramble
From Bennington to Burlington, Vermont (125 miles)
Step back into small-town America and experience ice-cream parlors, general stores, covered bridges, and trout fishing.
Best time to go: summer or fall

Car Travel

Costs to Consider

Fuel

Wear: Added mileage/automo-
  bile *depreciation*

Tear: Repair costs for any dents,
  dings, and damage to car

Auto insurance

Lodging and meals during overnight stays on the road

Parking fees and *tolls*

Conveniences

Make your own schedule/set
  your own pace

Have a car at destination

Leave from and return to your
  home; arrive directly at destination

Divide expenses among passengers

No long waits or lengthy security checks at airports

Transport more baggage and gear

Benefits

Enjoy the scenery

Stop at points of interest

Take interesting *side-trips*

Keep feet on the ground, get out and stretch legs, breathe fresh air

Depreciation

The drop in an item's value that occurs over time.

Toll

A fee that's paid to drive on a road or cross over a bridge.

Side-trip

A short or brief trip that isn't part of the main itinerary.

Air Travel

Costs to Consider

Airfare

Ground transportation to and
from airports

Tips for people who help with
baggage

Baggage fees (for some airlines,
checked and/or carry-on)

Individual fares for travel companions

Snacks during long airport waits/meals aboard plane

Conveniences

SPEED! It's the fastest way to go!

Less time to take off from work/be away from home

No route planning needed

No car to park in crowded cities

Beverages, meals, or snacks often served at your seat

Benefits

Lean back and relax/nap on the plane/arrive rested

Read, catch up on paperwork, watch a movie, or play a game

Ground transportation

The forms of transportation available to take passengers from the
airport to a nearby city. Examples include rental cars, taxicabs, and
limousines, as well as buses and trains.

Using Technology on the Plane

Many air travelers are surprised to learn that they are forbidden to use their cell phones while the plane is in the air. That's the law on all US flights. Other devices must be turned off from the time the cabin door closes until the plane reaches a level of 10,000 feet. While the plane is at that level, passengers can use laptop computers, MP3 players, DVD players, and electronic games. Some airlines provide Wi-Fi for a fee.

Forms of Airport Security

1. **Fences, *barriers*, and walls:** Today, airports are fully enclosed, and the outer edges are patrolled by guards around the clock. Areas where planes are fueled and baggage is handled have especially tight security.

   Barrier
   A structure that blocks entry.

   Screen
   To check for the purpose of protecting. When items are *screened*, the ones thought to be unsafe or unfit are removed.

2. **Traveler identification:** Domestic travelers must

carry a form of identification with a photo, such as a driver's license. International travelers must carry a passport. In the future, passengers may be **screened** further using fingerprints, eye scans, and other biological measures.

3. **Traveler screening:** To get into the gate area of the airport, passengers must pass through physical screening devices. Most airports use metal detectors and X-ray machines to screen passengers and the items they want to carry onto the plane.

4. **Baggage screening:** Baggage that is checked on the plane is also X-rayed. So is all of the cargo being shipped, including packages and mail. Dogs are used to sniff out explosives.

5. **Boarding restrictions:** Passengers can't take a number of materials onto the plane: explosives and weapons, household chemicals, spray containers, poisons, and corrosives (such as acids). Also, passengers acting suspicious or threatening can be prevented from boarding.

6. **Onboard security:** The door leading into the plane's cockpit is locked. This prevents anyone from entering the cockpit and taking over or interfering with the flying of the plane. US marshals are aboard many flights, although their identities are kept secret. Air marshals can carry guns and arrest people.

CHAPTER **4**

Choosing a Hotel or Motel: Luxury or Economy?

Hotel and Motel Ratings

Leo is ready to make a lodging ***reservation.*** He's gathered travel guides and checked Web sites that rate hotels, motels, resorts, and inns. The rating systems run from one star to five, with five being the highest:

→ Five-star ★ ★ ★ ★ ★ ***accommodations*** are often called "deluxe." They have elegant lobbies and luxurious rooms. They also have great locations and provide a range of top-level services.

Reservation

An arrangement made in advance to stay at a hotel for a desired number of nights.

Accommodations

The quality of the room and services provided by a hotel.

110

→ Three- ✶✶✶ and four-star ✶✶✶✶ hotels are generally called "first class." While they are still high quality, they are less luxurious and less expensive.

→ A one- ✶ or two-star ✶✶ rating usually goes to a budget motel. These places are often labeled "tourist class." They can be well run and provide great value. But they can also be downright shabby.

Considering the Options

Leo believes strongly in the saying "You get what you pay for." He's very interested in having the luxurious experience described on the next page. But he's also interested in value. He might select the budget-minded motel described on pages 113–114.

Leo Goes for Luxury

A uniformed doorman greets Leo and opens the door to the Parkside Grande, a five-star hotel. Leo walks across the thick carpet in the lobby and admires the expensive furniture. A beautiful fountain bubbles merrily. Gold-rimmed cups gleam at the ***complimentary*** coffee bar.

When a staff member carries Leo's bags to his room, Leo pays a tip. Soon, another employee delivers the snack Leo ordered from room service. Leo signs the bill and pays another tip.

Complimentary
Free of charge.

[FACT]

How Much to Tip at Hotels

- **Parking staff:** Tip the attendant who gets your car from the parking lot $2 to $5. Don't tip the person who puts your car in the lot or opens your door.
- **Bellmen:** Tip the bellman that carries your luggage $1 to $2 per bag. Tip more if the bags are heavy or the bellman provides other services.
- **Concierge/Guest Services:** Don't tip someone who just answers questions or gives directions. Do tip someone who gets tickets to a sold-out concert or a table at a popular restaurant. Tip him or her $10 to $50.
- **Maids:** Tip the maid $1 to $5 a day. Leave the tip in the room each day to make sure the person who does the work gets the money.

When Leo checked in, he was told to "dial 7" when he wants to use his car. A parking attendant will bring it around from the $15-a-night lot. To avoid tipping the attendant, Leo decides he will walk to dinner. Staying downtown means that fine restaurants and entertainment are nearby. Leo found a great restaurant by plugging in his laptop and using the room's free Wi-Fi service.

Leo Sticks to a Budget

When Leo enters the tidy lobby of the Econo-Stay Motel, he sees a table holding postcards, a coffee pot, and paper cups. He hears the constant sound of planes buzzing overhead. They arrive and depart from the nearby airport all day and night.

"Your room is ready," the desk clerk tells Leo. "Park anywhere in the lot. It's free. And help yourself to coffee, if you wish."

Leo carries his bags up the stairs and down the hall to room 214. It's small and well kept—just what he'd expected from a two-star motel. The Econo-Stay is part of a nationwide chain with a good reputation. It offers "no frills" comfort and cleanliness at an inexpensive price.

Leo buys a soda from the machine down the hall. After returning to his room, he looks in the phone book for restaurants. Then he turns up the air conditioner and flicks on the TV. He decides to take a refreshing rest before making the 20-minute drive downtown for dinner.

Top-Five Hotel Amenities

A 2010 survey of hotel guests asked for their "must-have" amenities. Here are the top five answers:

1. Wireless Internet access
2. Complimentary breakfast
3. Choices in bedding and pillows
4. Pillow-top mattress
5. Free parking

Making the Choice

To decide which features and **amenities** he needs, Leo used this checklist:

Amenities

Things that make people feel comfortable and at ease.

Hotel Features and Amenities

What's important to you?

- ☐ prime location
- ☐ large room
- ☐ air conditioning
- ☐ pets welcome
- ☐ free parking
- ☐ room service
- ☐ Wi-Fi or Internet access
- ☐ restaurants nearby
- ☐ free local phone calls
- ☐ elegant lobby
- ☐ discount/budget rates

- ☐ in-room movies
- ☐ airport transportation
- ☐ cable TV
- ☐ meeting facilities
- ☐ swimming pool
- ☐ refrigerator/microwave
- ☐ quiet
- ☐ handicapped accessible
- ☐ exercise/workout facilities
- ☐ safe and secure

Word List

abbreviation
acceptable
access
accommodations
accurate
acquaint
adjust
admire
advertise
advice
agency
alert
allocate
alternate
alternative
amenities
amusing
annual
anticipate
application
appointment
approximately
assaulted
assign
assist
associated
assume
attendant
attractions

baggage
bargain
barrier
biased
boarding
booking
boundary

breathless
brochure
budget
bureau

campus
cancel
carpool
celebration
certify
check-in
citizenship
cleanliness
co-worker
coaches
commute
complimentary
condition
confirmation
congestion
consequence
consistent
constant
continental
convenient
convince
costly
criminal
crosswalk
culture

dangerous
decrease
defensive
deluxe
demand
departure

designed
desire
destination
determine
device
disabilities
disaster
discount
disease
distance
document
domestic
drawback

economical
elderly
elegant
elevated
eligible
encourage
enthusiasm
environment
equality
equipment
especially
estimated
evidence
exception
exchange
expensive
experience
expire

federal
flexible
forbidden
forecast

foreign
formal
frustration
fuel
function

getaway
guidelines

hazard
highway
historical
hitchhiking
hometown

identical
identification
identity
immunization
indicate
inexpensive
interfering
international
intersection
interstate
interval
invisible
issued
itinerary

jeopardy

legend
leisure
light rail
locale
lodging
luxurious

Word List

maintain
maintenance
mass transit
media
medication
membership
mileage
miscellaneous
moderate
motorist
multiple

nationwide
nonrefundable
nonstop
normally

obstacle
obvious
occupant
off-season
onboard
ongoing
option
organization
outbreak

passenger
passport
patrolled
peak
pedestrian
performance
permission
personnel
persuade

policy
pollution
popularity
possibility
practical
predict
preference
priority
procedure
promote

qualify

readable
reasonable
receipt
recommend
recreation
refund
regional
regulation
reliable
relieve
renew
represent
reputation
reschedule
reservation
resources
responsibilities
restrict
risk
round trip
route

scenic
schedule

screen
security
seldom
seriously
sightseeing
similarity
situation
souvenir
specialize
specific
splurge
statistics
strain
stressful
stride
suburb
subway
support
survey
suspicious
symbol

tension
terminology
terrorist
threatening
thrifty
toll
tourist
transfer
transport
transportation
typical

unexpectedly
unique
unstable

update
urban

valuable
vary
vehicle
veteran
victim
vigorous
visible

Web site
widespread

yield

Index

AAA. *See* American Automobile Association

Acela, 68. *See also* High-speed trains

Air travel. *See* Plane

Airport codes, 77, 79. *See also* Itinerary

Amenities, at hotels, 114, 115. *See also* Lodging

American Automobile Association (AAA), 98–99

American Volkssport Association (VAA), 19

Amtrak, 66–67, 68. *See also* Train

Biking, 20–25
  benefits of, 25
  equipment for, 20, 21, 23, 25
  rules for, 20, 22–25
  safety of, 21, 22–25

Blogs, by travelers, 95. *See also* Web sites

Budget (travel), 98–103
  daily average for, 98–99
  example of, 100–101
  and lodging, 111, 113–114
  tips for, 102, 103

Bus (travel), 42–47, 48–53, 54–59
  benefits of, 41, 42–43
  cost of, 40, 41, 54–56
  history of, 36
  popularity of, 38, 39
  routes of, 42–47, 52–53

  safety of, 58, 59
  schedules for, 48–53, 57
  tips for, 57–58
  transfer for, 38, 58
  types of, 52–53

Car sharing, 26, 30, 31. *See also* Carpooling; Ride sharing

Car travel. *See* Driving

Carpooling, 26, 27–28. *See also* Ride sharing

Check-in, for flight, 80–81. *See also* Plane; Security

City bus lines, 52. *See also* Bus, routes of

College students
  bus passes for, 56
  ride sharing by, 13, 31
  train passes for, 67

Commuting, 26, 27. *See also* Car sharing; Carpooling; Ride sharing; Van pools

Confirmation number, for flight, 78. *See also* Itinerary

Cycling. *See* Biking

Defensive bike riding, 21, 22. *See also* Biking, safety of

Demand-responsive transit (DRT), 40, 41

Destination (travel), 92–97
  cost of, 99

high vs. low seasons for, 97

resources for selecting, 92, 93–96

Disabled individuals, travel by, 35, 57, 67

Domestic flight, 73, 74, 80. *See also* Itinerary

Driving (travel)
  benefits of, 104, 106
  cost of, 98, 104, 106
  vs. flying, 104, 106–107. *See also* Plane
  routes/trips for, 105
  time needed for, 104, 106

DRT. *See* Demand-responsive transit

Elevated train, 38. *See also* Train

Flying. *See* Plane

Food. *See* Meals

Friend, traveling with, 102

Greyhound Lines, 53

Guidebooks, 93–94, 95. *See also* Planning, resources for

Health issues, for overseas travel, 86

High-occupancy vehicle (HOV) lanes, 28

High season, for travel, 97

Index

High-speed trains, 68, 69. *See also* Train
Hitchhiking, 8–12
  dangers of, 8, 10–12, 13
  definition of, 9
  laws about, 10, 11
  popularity of, 9, 11
Hotels. *See* Lodging
HOV lanes. *See* High-occupancy vehicle (HOV) lanes

Immunizations, for overseas travel, 86
International flight, 73, 74, 80. *See also* Itinerary
Itinerary, for flight, 76–81. *See also* Plane
  changing of, 81
  definition of, 76
  example of, 77
  information on, 77–79, 81

Legend, of bus route map, 44, 45, 46–47
Light rail transit (LRT), 38–41. *See also* Train
Lodging, 110–115
  cost of, 98, 101, 103
  features of, 114, 115
  and tipping, 112
  types/ratings of, 110–111
Low season, for travel, 97
LRT. *See* Light rail transit

Mass transit, 36, 37, 48. *See also* Public transportation
Meals, cost of, 98, 101, 102, 103
Motels. *See* Lodging

National bus lines, 53. *See also* Bus, routes of
New York City, public transportation in, 36, 37, 38, 52

Overseas travel, 82–87
  health issues for, 86
  passport for, 82–85. *See also* Passport
  by plane, 73, 74, 80. *See also* Plane
  safety issues for, 87

Park & Ride, 43
Pass
  for bus travel, 40, 41, 54, 55, 56. *See also* Bus, cost of
  vs. ticket, 55, 56
  for train travel, 67
Passport, 82–85
  applying for, 82, 84–85
  cost of, 84
  expiration of, 86
  time needed for, 85
Peter Pan Bus Lines, 53. *See also* Regional bus lines

Plane (travel), 70–75, 76–81
  benefits of, 62–63, 104, 107
  check-in for, 80–81
  cost of, 62, 70, 71, 98, 101, 104, 107
  vs. driving, 104, 106–107. *See also* Driving
  itinerary for, 76–81. *See also* Itinerary
  restrictions for, 72, 74, 81
  security for, 80, 108–109
  technology use on, 108
  time needed for, 62–63, 80–81, 104, 107
  vs. train, 61, 62–63. *See also* Train
  types of fares/flights, 70–71, 72–75
Planning, of trip/vacation, 92–97, 98–103
  budget, 98–103. *See also* Budget
  resources for, 92, 93–96
  when to go, 97
  where to go, 92–97. *See also* Destination
Public transportation
  history of, 36, 37
  popularity of, 39
  schedules for, 48. *See also* Schedules
  types of, 36, 38–41. *See also* specific types

Index

Rail travel. *See* Train
Receipt, for flight, 76, 77.
   See also Itinerary
Regional bus lines, 52–53.
   See also Bus, routes
   of
Restrictions, for plane
   travel, 72, 74, 81. *See*
   also Plane
Ride sharing, 26–31
   availability of, 13, 30
   resources for, 29, 30
   types of, 26, 29, 30–31.
      See also Car sharing;
      Carpooling; Van pools
Route maps, for buses,
   44–47. *See also* Bus,
   routes of

Schedules
   for buses, 48–53
   example of, 50–51
   for public transportation,
      48
Security, for plane travel,
   80, 108–109
Shoes, for walking, 16, 19
Stretching, before walking,
   16, 18
Subway, 38
Symbols, on bus route
   map, 44, 45, 46–47

Technology use, on plane,
   108

Television programs, about
   traveling, 96. *See also*
   Planning, resources
   for
Ticket, vs. pass, 55, 56.
   See also Pass
Tipping, at hotels, 112. *See*
   also Lodging, cost of
Tourism bureaus, 96.
   See also Planning,
   resources for
Train (travel), 64–69
   benefits of, 62, 63,
      64–66
   cost of, 62, 67
   passes for, 67
   vs. plane, 61, 62–63
   popularity of, 38, 39
   time needed for, 62–63,
      66, 67, 68, 69
   types of, 38–41, 65, 68,
      69. *See also* Elevated
      train; Light rail transit;
      Subway
Transfer, and bus travel,
   38, 58. *See also* Bus,
   routes of
Travel warnings/alerts, for
   overseas trips, 87
Trip, planning of. *See*
   Planning

US Surgeon General, 15, 16

VAA. *See* American Volkssport Association

Vacation, planning of. *See*
   Planning
Van pools, 26, 30. *See also*
   Ride sharing
Visa, for travel, 85. *See*
   also Passport

Walking, 14–19
   benefits of, 15, 17
   clubs for, 19
   guidelines for, 16
   shoes for, 16, 19
   types of, 15, 17
Walking clubs, 19
Walking shoes, 16, 19
Web sites
   for planning a trip/
      vacation, 95
   for ride sharing, 29, 30
   for travel warnings/
      alerts, 87